Menorca

EVEREST

Photographs: Miguel Raurich
Lluis Bertrán (p. 18, 31, 34-35, 37b, 43, 44, 46a, 46b, 46c, 47, 50, 55, 64a, 64b)
Triangle (p. 32, 33a, 38, 62-63)

Layout: Gerardo Rodera

Cover design: Alfredo Anievas

Inselkarte: Francisco A. Morais

Translation: EURO:TEXT (Martin Gell)

SECOND EDITION
© EDITORIAL EVEREST, S.A.
Carretera León-La Coruña, km 5 - LEÓN
ISBN: 84-241-3632-2
Legal deposit: LE. 1.376-1998
Printed in Spain

EDITORIAL EVERGRÁFICAS, S.L.
Carretera León-La Coruña, km 5
LEON (Spain)

MENORCA (MINORCA)

Of the islands belonging to the Balearic archipelago, Minorca is the one that lies farthest to the north and to the east. Featuring a surface area of 702 km², it has approximately 60,000 inhabitants. The island's relief is one of gentle forms, comprising Primary and Triassic terrains in the north and Miocene limestones in the south, whilst its highest peak is that of Monte Toro (358 m). Its coastline is relatively unbroken, with the exception of the port of Mahón (or Maó).

The Minorcan climate is clearly of a Mediterranean nature, with average temperatures of around 17°C and annual rainfall figures of 575 mm. The north winds have given shape to a landscape which is lacking in woodland and abundant in plant-covered dunes.

The island scenery is dominated by scrubland featuring wild olives, mastic trees, heathers and cistuses, whilst its forested areas are limited to a series of small pine and holm oak woods. Most of the crops harvested here are obtained by dry farming, above all cereals and fodder crops used to maintain the local cattle, whose milk and meat constitute a vital factor of the island's economy. Industry on the island is devoted to dairy goods production (including the highly prestigious Mahón cheeses), the manufacture of shoes and imitation jewelry, and the distillation of liquors (mainly gin).

Tourism is equally as important here as it is throughout the archipelago, although Minorca does not have the same degree of mass tourism, focussing on less exploited areas such as hiking or horseriding holidays. Neither should it be forgotten that the island boasts coves of great beauty and an unrivalled archaeological heritage founded above all on its megalithic monuments (*taulas, navetas, talayots...*).

The most important towns on Minorca are Mahón, the capital, and Ciudadela, both of which warrant a comprehensive visit before one goes on to explore the beauties that the rest of the island holds in store.

View of Mahón.

Eastern sector of Mahón.

San Roc Gate. ▶

Mahón

According to tradition the name and foundation of Mahón is to be traced back to the Carthaginian General Magón, although it first achieved importance in Roman times as *Portus Magonis*, when use was made of the exceptional natural features of its inlet in order to afford shelter to vessels. This was an era of great prosperity for Mahón. Subsequently it became the dominion of Vandals and Byzantines until it was subjected to rule by the Moslems, the latter being expelled by King Alfonso III in 1286.

However, it was the British domination - and with it 18th-century trade and privateering - that brought about the true development of modern-day Mahón. In 1801 (the Treaty of Amiens), Mahón finally became part of Spain.

Ses Voltes and the Church of Santa María.
Two-page spread overleaf, sunset over Mahón port.

The nave and organ at Santa María la Mayor.

Plaza de la
Reconquista and
Mahón town
hall.

Modernist architecture on Minorca.

Casa Mir. ▶

Plaza del Carmen.

Mahón also preserves examples of modernist architecture such as the *Casa Mir.*

Other churches that are worth a visit are those of *San Francisco* and *El Carmen* (18th century).

Above all, Mahón is a town one can stroll around at ease, losing oneself in the peaceful streets that exude a typically Balearic character.

Casa Ulldemolins.

Things to See in Mahón

The following points of interest constitute the principal artistic attractions in Mahón:

— *Iglesia de Santa María.* Originally 13th-century, this church was rebuilt in the 18th. It features an aisleless nave and a 17th-century processional cross attributed to the Catalan silversmith P.Marcer.

— *The Town Hall.* Dating from the early 17th century, this building underwent extensive alterations in 1789.

— *Fine Arts Museum.* Contains important archaeological remains from all over the island.

— *Remains of the Castle of San Felipe* (18th century).

— *Georgetown District.* The British converted this former poor area into a typically British residential district, which subsequently was to be widely imitated.

The Golden Farm.

The Golden Farm
This is the name (Sp.: *La Granja Dorada*) given to the old farmhouse at Sant Antoni, to the north of the port of Mahón. It is also called *Casa de Nelson* due to the fact that Admiral Nelson once stayed here on a visit to Minorca.
At present the farmhouse is privately owned and contains period furniture and an extensive library with a large number of volumes on the subject of the legendary British admiral, some of whose personal effects are also kept here.

Café in Mahón.

Mahón fishmarket.

Two views of Mahón.

An artist attempts to capture the beauty of Mahón.

Cala Binisafulla. ▶

Southern Minorca

The southern part of the island affords the visitor beautiful coves such as Binibeca, Coves, Binisafulla, Macarella, Macarelleta and El Porter, beaches such as that of Son Bou and interesting towns like Ferreries.

Binibeca Vell is a fishing village built in traditional Minorcan fashion. Its geometrically shaped, small windowed, whitewashed houses provide a unique backdrop for strolls around secluded streets, passageways, arches and squares. Taken as a whole, this village is of great beauty.

Below, Cala Binisafulla.
On the facing page and
overleaf, two views of
Binibeca Vell.

Facing page,
Binibeca Vell.

Cala En Porter.

Nestling in **Cala En Porter** is the picturesque **Cueva d'en Xoroi**, a cave which is reached by means of steps carved out from the cliffs. Although prehistoric vessels have been found here, the most renowned legend attributed to the cave is that of its having been used as a hiding place by a Moor called Xoroi upon his abducting a Christian maiden.

*Cala Coves and, above these lines,
Cova d'en Xoroi.*

Cala En Porter.

Son Bou Beach.

Ferreries. ▶

Livestock in the proximity of Ferreries.

Although **Ferreries** is today the perfect place from which to set out for tourist spots such as **Santa Galdana beach** and **Cala Mitjana**, it is also of considerable historical interest, since its records go back as far as the 13th century. Under British rule it was an important junction on the route from Mahón to Ciudadela. Nowadays Ferreries has largely given up its traditional farming activity to focus on tourism, taking advantage of its marvellous position and beautiful scenery. The town boasts numerous excellent restaurants.

View of Ferreries.

The vicinity of Es Migjorn Gran.

Cala Mitjana.   *Cala Galdana.*   *Cala Macarella.* ▶

Cala Macarella.

Between the coves of Santa Galdana and En Turqueta lie those of **Macarella** and **Macarelleta**; both feature clear waters and beaches of fine sand. Other attractions are to be found in the surrounding area, such as megalithic remains and a prehistoric well.

The rural hermitage of **Sant Joan de Missa** is situated five kilometres from Ciudadela. In all probability it was built subsequent to the conquest of the island in 1287. The St John's Day vigil held here is attended by the horsemen participating in the *fiestas de Sant Joan* in Ciudadela.

Ciudadela

The origins of this town are to be traced back to a Roman settlement that was later occupied by the Moslems. Upon the conquest of Minorca by Christian forces, Ciudadela was chosen as its capital. Even though capital status was transferred to Mahón in 1722, Ciudadela still remains the religious heart of the island.

On the preceding page,
Ciudadela port. This page,
Ciudadela cathedral.

Ciudadela was traditionally the seat of the island's aristocracy, a fact borne witness to by a large number of surviving stately homes situated within what were once the town walls, demolished in 1873.
The ancient *Real Alcázar*, formerly the residence of Moorish and Christian kings, now acts as the local town hall.
The streets of Ciudadela, many of which are arcaded, retain the character of times gone by and are the ideal place for a pleasant stroll. One such street is the renowned **'Ses Voltes'**, of a markedly Arab nature.

Above and on facingç page, two views of Plaça des Born.
The following two-page spread, Ciudadela by night.

Ciudadela Cathedral is Gothic in style and was begun in 1300. Also noteworthy is the Iglesia del Rosario, a church dating from the 18th century and featuring a beautiful baroque façade. The episcopal palace, today Neoclassical in stye, was originally Gothic.
Amongst the most important tourist attractions of Ciudadela are the **fiestas de Sant Joan**, the local festivities in which over a hundred horsemen in traditional dress perform equestrian feats of medieval origin.
The port of Ciudadela still retains a bustling fishing industry.

On the facing page, night-time and festive views of Ciudadela.
This page, the renowned Festes de Sant Joan.

Dusk over the port of Ciudadela.

Cala Morell and its prehistoric caves.

◀ *Cala Pilar.*   *Cala Pregonda.*

At the heart of the island is the town called **Es Mercadal**, a beautiful tourist resort famed for its specialities in confectionery. Es Mercadal lies at the foot of Monte Toro, at 358 metres the highest mountain on Minorca. From Monte Toro one can enjoy an impressive view of the whole island. Situated here is the **sanctuary** at which the image of *'Mare de Deu'*, the patron saint of Minorca, is venerated. Pilgrimage to the sanctuary is undertaken with great devotion by the islanders. From Es Mercadal one can reach the towns of **Migjorn Gran** and **Alaior**, the latter featuring a fortified parish church.

Left, a view of the north coast with the Island of Porros facing us. Below, Fornells port. On the facing page, the lighthouse at Cap de Cavalleria.

On the facing page, above: Cap de Favaritx; below, the Alaior parish church.
Above these lines, S'Albufera.

Setting out from Es Mercadal we can also follow the route along the northern coast that leads us to an area comprising the following spots: the village of **Sanitja**, a harbour that still preserves remains of the ancient Roman settlement and whose coastal scenery is of immense beauty; the **Cap de Cavalleria**, the northernmost point of the island, with its lighthouse, from which the spectacular northern coastline and the Island of Porros can be seen; and the town of **Fornells**, a strategic settlement that was fortified as early as the 17th century, further defensive structures having been erected under British rule. Today Fornells is a fishing village that offers delicious seafood cuisine.

Es Mercadal and Monte Toro.
Above, the sanctuary entrance.

Archaeological Minorca

One of the major attractions of the island is its profusion of past remains, unique in Spain and even within the Balearic Islands. The most characteristic of these remains are those of megalithic origin, such as the *taulas*, *navetas* and *talayots*, built using enormous stone blocks and whose function and purpose are still a mystery.

Amongst these monuments we should highlight the following: **Torre d'en Gaumés**, the most important prehistoric settlement on Minorca, a complex of *taulas, talayots* and a hypostyle; **Taula de Torralba**, a stone's throw from Alaior, the largest and best-carved *taula* on the island; **Talatí de Dalt**, situated near Mahón, a complete megalithic settlement whose outstanding feature is its monumental *taula*; the great **Talayot de Torrellonet**, close to the airport, so well-preserved that one can still see the large window on its upper section; the **Taula and Talayot of Trepuco**, which together make up what is perhaps the most representative ensemble on Minorca; and finally the **Naveta d'es Tudons**, on the outskirts of Ciudadela, a great Bronze Age pantheon divided into two floors.

Torre d'En Gaumés.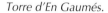

Taula de Torralba. ▶

Talatí de Dalt.

The **Palaeochristian Basilica of Son Bou**, situated in the sandy area of the same name, was built over the 5th and 6th centuries, thus bearing witness to the deep-rooted Christian tradition on Minorca. Its remains point to the existence of a building that was as solid as it was humble, comprising a nave and two aisles crowned by a semicircular apse. Still surviving today is the monolithic, massive baptismal font, circular in shape and featuring a cross-shaped cavity.

Palaeochristian Basilica of Son Bou.

Talayot at Torrellonet Vell.

Above, Naveta d'Es Tudons.
Opposite, Trepuco taula.

Two scenes of traditional Minorca culture: a wickerwork craftsman and typical island folklore.